I Didn't used to BE THIS way

I Didn't used to BE THIS way

LOUISE CASE

Charleston, SC
www.PalmettoPublishing.com

I Didn't Used To Be This Way

Copyright © 2021 by Louise Case

All rights reserved

No portion of this book may be reproduced,
stored in a retrieval system, or transmitted in any form
by any means–electronic, mechanical, photocopy, recording,
or other–except for brief quotations in printed reviews,
without prior permission of the author.

First Edition

Paperback ISBN: 978-1-63837-986-7
eBook ISBN: 978-1-63837-987-4

Everyone in this book has changed my life somehow. I can't really dedicate this to just one person. Thanks to the stay-at-home moms that mothered me. Thanks to my brother and his friends who had a bigger hand in raising me than they realize. Thanks to family who loved me even when I wasn't very loveable. Thanks to the friends that turned out to be family. Thanks to my "stand-in dad" Jack, and Kathy, who will forever be my parents, and Cate, whom I proudly call my sister. Thanks to Kayla and our childhood–after college friendship and all that she did for me when others would have just walked right on by. Last but certainly not least, thanks to Ms. D, for without her, I'd have never been a nurse, let alone on this planet. Thanks to anyone who took time to read this. I hope it helps someone.

Nursing school is hard. It doesn't matter which one you go to, or what kind of nurse you're studying to be, it just is. You learn a lot in the classroom and clinicals, but it's the "life-ing" that goes on around you while you're stressed to the max that really teaches you how to survive in this world. Your family life takes a beating, your romantic relationships become non-existent, and the only "friends" that you really see are the friends that you've made in class that are going through the same or similar struggles that you are. You get real good at internally falling apart while on the outside you look like you've got your shit together. You get good at going on autopilot. Emotions? Never heard of her. Most had a vice like partying and drinking to the point of puking or hooking up with someone at a party that you don't know. We all do what we have to do to get through this part of life. Until one day, you just don't. The bottom falls out, and no one is going to catch you.

In our intro class, we were told all of this and more. (Especially now that they had our money. No turning back now.) So many "Nancy Nurses" were ready to take on the world and make it better. They had no idea how by the end of the program that your outlook on life would change so drastically. Clinicals had a great way of making you lose faith in humanity in general.

Just think…We were only wearing patches at this point, so it was the "real nurses" that truly had to deal with it. Don't get me wrong; students took their fair share of bullshit. If we were lucky…big if…we got to follow a nurse that liked to teach, and they generally would watch out for us. Some just watched us and let us drown. If you get nothing more from this book, if you're a nurse that precepts: Don't be a bitch. Read that again. You were once a baby nurse that didn't know anything. Sure, you passed the NCLEX, but that is just false hope that you knew what to do. Once your feet hit the floor, everything goes out the window. You have no idea what you're doing. Be a nurse you'd want to work with. Help them. Give them breaks to go cry when they are overwhelmed. Don't forget that most things we were taught on a dummy, and we know the "textbook" way to do things. Teach them the "real way" to do things. The way you do it when you're given too many patients, and it seems like everything is on fire. Pass on your tricks, your time savers… teach them how to take care of the patient well and efficiently. Remember, we've had our noses in books for almost two years. We know nothing. We are newly licensed sponges. We are going to learn by watching and doing. We are just as lost as you were when you first started this thing we'll call a career. Remember that.

We were told that out of our small class of 15, at least two relationships would fail; we would all struggle with family and to buy our uniforms a size up due to the studying/stress eating. Oh yeah, and then they sneak in the, "At least one of you will get pregnant." Most of these were correct. Actually, during the program, they were pretty spot on. (I ended up losing weight during the program, but keep reading and you'll put it together.)

I moved from my tiny hometown (two stop lights and a Walmart at the time). My senior year was hellish. While most were partying and really enjoying their last year, I was home-schooled and had had brain surgery. I'm talking about major surgery that the surgeon basically told me that I'd throw a clot and would never make it off the table. Pretty scary to swallow at 18 years old. Obviously, I made it off the table because I'm here to write about it. Another nursing tidbit: most specialists are dickheads that have a God complex. It doesn't matter if you're working with them or you're their patient. They have a talent that not many possess and have gone to school for years and years. I get it. You want someone that is going into your brain to be confident. There's a fine line between being confident and being cocky. Most specialists ride that line.

In my little town, there are two state universities that parents send their kids to. One is about 45 minutes away and is more of an agricultural school; one is about two hours away, and it seems to focus on everything else. I didn't get to go to either of these. My dad was a butcher with a gambling problem, and my mom was a nurse that always put work ahead of the family, except for when I got sick. That was the first and only time I can remember her taking off work to take care of one of her kids. She was so career and money driven that honestly, she should have never had kids. It wasn't until my brother and I were both adults that she admitted that, then conveniently forgot and denied it was ever said. If Ben hadn't been there, I'd have probably somehow made myself think that I had dreamt it. Growing up she used to joke that I should have been in a jar, and it took me a few years to figure out that was her abortion joke. I was always the "accident." That never really bothered me. My dad always said I was his baby girl, so it seemed to balance everything out in my head. She later found Jesus and conveniently forgot she ever said it. She forgot a lot of what she said and did. It's funny how people find a higher power when they're circling the bowl and don't want to think of the idea that you're laid in the ground and slowly became worm food. So the idea of going to heaven was much easier to swallow, especially when she smoked herself into lung disease and worked herself into a wheelchair. She was so focused on being the best nurse, she didn't stop and take care of herself. She literally worked out of an electric wheelchair the last couple of years before she finally had to retire.

My brother, Ben, was cursed to be first born and missed out on a lot to take care of me. (He also took a lot of physical abuse that was meant for me.) Mom liked to hit. Moreover, she wanted to see us cry. Ben and I both got to the point where we wouldn't cry. We'd be damned if we would give her the satisfaction of seeing tears. Our grandma helped out a lot, but she only knew about half of the story. We knew better than to talk about it. We both had a couple of friends that were allowed to come into the house, and they were sworn to secrecy. Our house wasn't in great condition. The kitchen was literally coming off the house; it seemed like Dad had rigged the foundation with jacks somehow, but I'm not completely sure of that. We had a basement that constantly flooded and had to be pumped out, making our yard a soggy mess that you really couldn't play in. Ben had a room, and Dad had a room. My mom usually slept on the couch, and I had a makeshift room in our walk-through den. I mostly slept with dad anyway. Ben was the oldest, so he of course got the other room. He also somehow worked full time at a fast food place and went to school. His grades weren't perfect, but if he had had more encouragement, he would have been a straight A student. He was in FFA and was really good at public speaking, a trait that I think he still uses to this day that works to his advantage. He is honestly one of the smartest people that I know. I'm talking about med school smart. I remember being heartbroken when he moved out as soon as he turned 18. I couldn't blame him though.

We didn't have a normal brother/sister relationship. Ben kind of raised me. That was good and bad in many ways. I was so proud when people asked me if I was his little sister. There was a lot of stability there, as much as a kid himself could give. He's four years older than me, but once he started driving, I was usually riding shotgun. He got married at 21 to someone pretty close to my age. I didn't like her—I mean I *really* didn't like her. (I'm not too proud to admit there was jealousy there.) I tried for a while to be nice, but that eventually went out the window. She graduated in May, and they got married in June. This was again when my jealousy reared its ugly head. Everything I did that day, I did for my brother. If I could've gotten away with it, I would have dyed her veil blue. However, the groomsmen had grown up with me and patted me down before I could get into the church. I was the bigger person for my brother, and did her hair and makeup. She actually looked pretty that day. (I'm not saying she was ugly: she wasn't. I'm just saying I did a good job.) However, being the shithead 16 year old that I was, I was sure to tell her that I could lock my legs while we were all up there, and if I passed out, he'd stop the wedding and go to the hospital with me. She knew I was right. All she said was, "Please don't." I didn't, but I just wanted to keep her on her toes and let her know who had the upper hand. I also told her with a smile on my face in a half hug—you know, the kind where your mouth is right by her ear—and whispered, "If you remember nothing from this day, I want you to remember these words: I was here before you, and I'll be here after you." There's actually a picture of it, and for those who don't know what I said, it looks very "sisterly." It was a small wedding in the Baptist church. Dad proudly wore his boutonniere and was in every picture he was asked to be in.

Mom bitched the whole time and just generally embarrassed him the whole damn day with shitty comments she would say and make sure others that had come could hear. "I don't know why they're even having this wedding…They've been fucking for months." Nice things like that. The kicker of the whole day was she refused to be in any pictures. He had to cry for her to stand in the back of one "family" photo to get her to do it, and my grandma had to shame her. Looking back, I'm glad I didn't dye the veil blue. My mother was being a big enough bitch for the both of us. I wasn't happy about it, but I supported it because he had always supported anything that I wanted to do. (He paid for most of it if he could even.)

My family was considered lower middle class at best. Mom worked all the time, although she mostly had salary jobs that required her to be on call 24/7. She complained about it a lot, but honestly, I think she thrived from it. At work, she knew what to do, and her word was law. She knew state regulations, and she hired and fired as she pleased. At home, my dad always seemed to be gone, so he didn't piss her off as much. She seemed to be overwhelmed and angry a lot. She was especially angered by my brother. They were like nails on a chalkboard to each other. Ben had no respect for her (I get that), and she had no trust or faith in Ben. It got to the point where he'd purposely piss her off. I just tried to stay out of the way. I went to the doctor for my first bleeding ulcer because of stress at the age of eight. It took me a long time to get tough. Nerves were something I had to acquire; I definitely wasn't born with them. Between Ben and me, we had kept that house running for as long as I can remember. Then, on her birthday, he asked her what she wanted. The response was, "You outta this house!" I was destroyed because I knew that he would do it, and then that would leave me there alone. We took care of each other. I made food, and he made sure stuff that I couldn't reach was dusted. He took out the trash and he was always allowed to use the stove. I got to where I could make anything in the microwave, then I'd cheat and use the stove as long as he was home.

He was out within the next week, and I was left to fend for myself. I went over to his place as much as my mom would let me, but using control as a punishment, it was a toss up whether I got to go or not. I'd do all the chores on the list and be done, then she'd come up with more things to do. So, I'd do those, and she'd finally let me go.

It was a very minimal apartment: mattress on the floor, a tv, closet with clothes, a VCR, and one video, "Independence Day" with Will Smith. I'm 38 years old and haven't seen it in years, but I could probably tell you most of that movie, word for word, because we had watched it so much. This was back when we could rent movies, but that took money, and every penny that Ben had either went to that tiny apartment, or to his car that he was always tinkering with. I think it was soothing for him. God knows, he deserved something for himself.

My brother had a couple of best friends, and looking back, I could see them becoming truly good guys. They never questioned me being right in the yard listening to them work on the car, learning new cuss words. (I said that they were growing into good guys, not perfect.) In my head, they were pretty perfect though. No one ever questioned taking me to eat with them or working on cars while I sat in one of the seats. One of his friends could literally spray paint a car, and it looked like the real deal. Every friend had their own talents when it came to cars. Had I had it to do all over again, I'd have had them teach me what they were doing instead of listening to the gossip and cuss words. My car was always taken care of by one of the guys, my brother, or my dad.

PSA to all the big brothers and dads who might read this: Don't assume that she knows what to check on her car if you've always done it. I knew where to put the gas, and I knew how to put windshield wiper fluid in. So, when I ran the oil out of my car in my early twenties, my dad really shouldn't have been as irate as he was. "Do you think the fucking oil-fairy comes and fills that shit up?!" Some fairy had been doing it my whole driving life; I didn't know I needed to check it. Also, to the girls who leave home with a car: If there's a grindy sound when you use your brakes, this is bad. In my defense, I'd tried to tell people, but life gets busy and people forget until you can't stop. Keep reading for all my life tidbits that I have, sometimes painfully, lived through. Also, before you leave for school, have someone get you a AAA card. This would have saved me from so many stressful moments.

If you don't have AAA (just get it), and you are going to school in an agricultural town, look for big-ass pickup trucks and cowboy boots. Those guys will rarely leave you stranded; most of them have manners and think and even say, when you offer to pay them with your very last $20, that if their little sister were in trouble, they would want someone to help her just like they were helping me. (I'm going to add here, my dad was an avid gun collector, and a flashbang holster can't even be seen on us girls with curvier frames. I never had any professional lessons, but I've shot many pop cans. Good enough to be confident that I could shoot small things from decently far away.) No victim mentality in this girl. That is, by far, my most hated word. Victim. It even pisses me off just typing it. Crazy shit can happen, but I'm not defined by it. (Remember this part.)

Let's talk about my dad for a minute. Like I said, he was a butcher with a gambling problem. He processed deer for everyone during hunting season and would mostly get paid with part of the deer he processed. Our freezer was always full when we didn't have much else. He hung out after work at the local taxidermist's place. That man could do some really cool stuff. I'm a butcher's daughter, so I looked at it as artistry. It was nothing for me to see dead animal carcasses hanging upside down out in the garage. I remember getting upset one time, and Dad explained it was the same stuff we bought at the grocery store, and that he wasted very little. Another reason why it made sense that his good friend was a taxidermist. What Dad didn't use, he did.

My dad was a really great cook. I honestly can't remember anything he did that turned out bad. Once a year, he would make homemade enchiladas. It was an all day process. I loved the sauce he made. He delivered plates to so many people in our little town. I remember the police driving by and turning their lights on, and he'd bring them out a plate too. He always said it was because he grew up poor, and he had to learn how to make little things taste good. Everything was fried though. When hunting season was over and our freezer was empty, no one knew this. My dad would've, and had, given his last dollar to help others, especially children and animals. I can't count how many times his back seat was weighed down with *almost* expired (although they were fine) lunch meats and meat from the counters. We did keep some, but most went to everyone else that was struggling.

Dad always seemed to be busy and was gone as much as he could be. I can't say I blamed him, but he had kids at home who were feeling the same way, and they had to have permission to leave that they rarely got. Later we found out that when he said he was going to a friend's place, he was gambling. He had hidden it pretty well until a credit card company called the house, and my mom answered it. All hell broke loose. Dad had a briefcase that was locked, and evidently it was where he kept all kinds of receipts from things he gambled on. I really don't remember what he gambled on, but I remember them screaming at each other. I've never been good with my nerves; Ben was the strong one, so right before I fell apart in front of them, Ben grabbed me and we went to his bedroom. We still heard everything, but it gave me a few minutes to try to collect myself. Ben threw me a magazine and said. "Act normal!" Sure. At that point, I was trying not to throw up. I heard Dad coming down the hall and opened the door. "Are you okay?" He half yelled, half spoke. I looked up from the magazine and just nodded my head with tears in my eyes, and my chest was already starting to hive—it's my tell. I heard him yell down the hall to my mom, "I suppose she's gonna need therapy, and that's gonna be my fault too!" Truth be told, Ben and I should have been in therapy years before that, and not from Dad. Mom could make existing hard. You were either in the way or not cleaning what and how she wanted. It was harder for me to hide, because my bedroom was the walk-through den.

I asked my grandma one day why Mom was the way she was. She told me that it didn't have anything to do with me… that some people didn't have the same capacity to love, and she thought Mom was one of them. She also said that my grandpa had been an alcoholic when she was little, and she thought maybe that had affected her ability to love. Grandma was one of the most godly women I've ever met; I knew she wasn't lying to me. Mom just must not have had a big enough capacity to love, and it wasn't Ben's or my fault. Thinking back, it must have been horrible for my grandma to have her eight-year-old granddaughter ask her why her mom didn't love her. I will say she handled it better than anyone else I knew. She let me know I could always come to her, and I got to see my cousins there. It was the truth, but I didn't want Grandma to know everything that was going on at home. There was no need to worry her.

During my school years, I tried to stay after school for something or go to my friend's house to work on homework. We were "latchkey kids," and if I had somewhere to go, that meant that my brother could go do things and didn't have to stay home with me, which he rarely griped about, but I know it was tough on him. His friends got to go places and do things, and he was stuck with me most days.

Hannah's mom was a stay-at-home mom, and most of the time, I got to stay for dinner. I was always impressed with her dinners because they had vegetables too. Hannah's mom, Julia, was what I called glamorous because she always had makeup on. She came to all of the classroom parties with homemade stuff. She wore cute clothes and had beautiful jewelry. I still attribute my love of makeup and perfume to her. She'd let us play with her makeup; I was much more interested than Hannah, and I just got to be a kid while I was over there. She's the reason that, to this day, I invest in good skin care and have eye cream by my bed in case I forget to put it on after my serums. (I told you skincare and makeup is my jam.)

Sometimes she'd give me little things like free gifts that she'd get from buying makeup while it was on special. Saying that it made my day can't adequately describe it. She had given me treasures. For almost thirty years, I have always remembered when she came home one day from a trip to Tulsa. She would often bring both Hannah and me treats. Never did she buy her something unless I got something too. She bought me a real, full size Lancome lipstick called Metallique. It was a light color, and I wore it until they discontinued it. I wore it when I took my nursing state boards, when I'd start a new job, or a new chapter of my life. It was my good luck charm! I dug out enough of the color with a Q-tip to put the color on my lips. My mom wore scrubs, and I can count on one hand how many times she wore makeup. Most of the time someone had died, or State was in the facility she worked at doing an audit. Julia was the first person, other than my grandma, that invested in me as a person. I know I was a kid chronologically, but I grew up fast and I think she saw that. Sometimes, I'd ask her how she cooked certain dishes, and how much things cost, because in my head I was trying to figure out if we could afford it and how I could possibly cook it in the microwave. Our funds were limited, but if it wasn't really expensive, I could ask my dad to bring it home from the grocery store. I was an old soul and was completely happy to talk about recipes. I could put a full meal on the table by the time I was eight. It's nothing to brag about; it was out of necessity. I never knew who was going to be home or when. Now, I always knew I could call my grandma, and she'd come and get me if I got scared, but I had to decide whether having Grandma come and get me outweighed havine my parents pissed because I "was fine."

Somehow I ended up staying the night the Friday before Easter. Hannah's family sat at a table for dinner together—sitting at the table blew my mind! They'd talk about all kinds of stuff. Our table was used as a catch-all; I don't ever remember sitting at the table together. With my family, it was probably a good thing. We just made plates, usually of mac and cheese or Ramen noodles. If we could swing it, I'd cook some chicken and chop it up like real soup, and then we went to our rooms to watch TV alone. I thought that's what everyone did. That Friday, Julia did their "normal" thing and asked everyone about school. I was glad it was over for the week, and Hannah and I had all night to play.

"What do you guys do for Easter, Lou?" Julia asked.

"Umm, I think everyone is working so Ben and I will probably watch TV. I might make deviled eggs. Grandma usually brings us a couple of dozen, and that's a good way to use them. Everyone likes them."

Julia kinda made a face, like I had either said something wrong or she didn't understand me. "You don't do Easter egg hunts and get Easter baskets?" she asked carefully.

I shoveled a fork full of salad in my mouth. I didn't usually have salads, and she had even made the Ranch dressing. "Well, we used to do that when I was little. (I was maybe eight at this point—again, old soul here), but no, Mom and Dad both work. Last year Ben hid some eggs for me to find, but I guess I didn't find them all, and it made the house smell. So we'll probably just watch cartoons maybe."

Again, Julia made that face like I might've said something wrong. I had to watch getting too comfortable. If I said the wrong thing, someone might take Ben and me away. "How do you make Ranch that doesn't come in a bottle?" I was nervously trying to change the subject because I thought maybe that had gotten me into trouble.

Hannah knew what I was trying to do and tried to help me. "I don't know, but it's really good!" We finished eating, and everyone helped clean up. Just before Hannah and I were getting ready to go jump on the trampoline, Julia called me from the living room. The house was decorated so pretty. Dark cherry wood and the couch was a cream color with a cranberry and dark green plaid pattern going through it. She was sitting in the cranberry color chair when I got into the living room. Hannah was sneaking out the back door to warm up the trampoline.

"Would you like to stay both nights this weekend with us? Do you think your mom and dad would care?" My parents were usually relieved if we found places to go. Mom always worked, and Dad worked and did whatever Dad did.

"I can call and ask. I don't think anyone would care." She handed me the cordless phone, and I got permission. That night we slept out on the trampoline and played outside most of the next day. We got to use fancy bath beads that turned our bathwater purple that night, and Julia braided my hair like she did Hannah's. I didn't know how to braid; I knew how to put my hair back in a ponytail and keep the tangles out though.

"If you go to bed with your hair braided and it's still kinda wet, it looks curly when you take it down." Hannah said like she was teaching a lesson. We giggled until we fell asleep.

Her brother was the first one to wake up. "The Easter Bunny has been here!" he yelled. I knew there was no such thing as one, but I didn't say anything.

We all filed into the living room, and there were Easter baskets. I was looking to see what Hannah had gotten, and Julia said, "Hey Lou…you got one too." She smiled. I didn't really know how to act. It had candy and girly things. Bonnie Bell lip smackers were my favorite. It took me a minute to process while the rest of the kids dug into theirs. She had done that for me. While Hannah and I were having a giggle-fest in her room, she was making me a basket. To most people, that wouldn't have been any big deal—but I. Got. A. Basket.

Sunday's were always kinda sad for me. It meant the week started over, and I had to go back to my life. When I got home, I remember my mom asking me what I had. "I got an Easter Basket." I saved Ben some candy so I was telling them about the weekend. My dad listened and seemed excited for me and even stole a malt ball.

"I'll get some candy when it's marked down in a couple of days," my mom mumbled as she went to the bedroom to watch TV.

We can go ahead and add my physical appearance now. I always had reddish hair, lots of freckles, and I was fat. Genetics played a factor in this. The women on my mom's side were all big, but we also ate what was cheap: Ramen noodles, the cheap mac 'n cheese, bologna, cheap white bread. Big bags of cereal, macaroni, and tomatoes, etc. Basically all the shit carbohydrates. That being said, I learned to be funny. It was a defense mechanism—tease myself before anyone else does. Most of the time it worked. It was a combination of that and being known as my brother's little sister; I didn't get messed with too much. Ben has always been a big guy, and he had a temper inherited from my dad and his Irish genes. I don't think he's ever backed down from a fight. It used to scare the hell out of me. I can't remember how old I was, maybe 12, and he was in a bad fight. Ever see your hero get hit in the face and kicked in the stomach? Mind you, he gave better than he got, but I had guys his age holding me back because I was going to kick this guy's ass, whoever he was. It was after the fight (he won), that my nerves had had it; we made a deal that he wouldn't fight in front of me if he could help it. Twenty years later, he still honors this. Once, about fifteen years ago, he came to a screeching halt and told me to get out and go to the park, and he'd pick me up soon. Yep…he was about to beat the brakes off someone, and he knew I couldn't take it. I grew up around more violence than I care to admit. Ben was who I ran to. To this day, I can't watch him fight. It kills me. Luckily, he calmed way down in his late thirties, early forties, but my stomach aches just thinking about him being violent. I know that's a learned trait. We saw it, and we emulated it. I'd be lying if I said I've never thrown a punch, but very few and when I do, I'm at my breaking point. Remember…I'm the funny one. I will hammer you with sarcasm before I put hands on you.

Back to nursing school… I knew there was no way that I'd ever be able to leave that little town and go to school unless I was able to figure out how to fund a big chunk of it myself. It's hard to save for college when you're babysitting to pay for groceries and air conditioning. One summer we really didn't get to run our window units, and Oklahoma summers are the armpit of hell. It didn't do well for Mom's mood either because somehow this was my dad's fault.

I earned some scholarships, one pretty sizable one, and my parents used their income tax return to pay for what they could. I worked to help pay what I could, but it wasn't much. I worked at a gym doing childcare. I was also a private nanny to a preemie baby boy who became attached to my hip a good part of the time. I lived in an efficiency close to the tech school that I attended. It was "all bills paid," so I knew exactly how much I needed every month. My brother paid to get me basic cable because he knew that I was more comfortable staying in and watching TV instead of going out. Most of the time, this was true.

Curriculum was a nightmare. Tests didn't match up with textbooks. I was in a "learn as you go" program. We were the first class to try this, and there were so many bugs to work out that we suffered through. I desperately needed lectures to understand the material, and I didn't have many teachers that would answer many questions, let alone lecture. I had one instructor that I still keep in touch with to this day: Ms. D. I still say I want to be her when I grow up. (I'm not sure when that'll be considering I'm 38 and still can't get my shit right.) When I met Ms. D, she was in her late fifties, working on her master's. A real spit fire with short red hair: I could tell she came from a small town and that Irish temper of hers was brewing most days. She fought for me from the start. She knew I studied my ass off and still wasn't getting it. She was the first one in all of the schooling I had had so far to tell me she thought I had a learning disability. She stayed late for one-on-one, and it really helped. I'll say this many times, but, without her (and my lipstick), I would not have passed my program, let alone my state boards.

I made two friends during the program, Lauren and Laney. Both seemed put together on the outside, but they were falling apart just as much as I was on the inside… and they were becoming weekend partying people. I really hadn't been able to do much in high school because I had been so sick. If it hadn't been for Kayla, my best friend in high school, I probably would've missed out on everything. She bought my senior packet for me (cap, gown, yearbook, memory book) and always tried to sneak a call from the bus on Senior trips. I did, however, miss out on the partying that all highschoolers got to to do, so this was new to me.

Thursday nights were the big party nights there. I guess it was because everyone tried to go home on Friday nights for the weekends. Lauren went through a divorce during the program. (See? They were right.) Laney had a toddler and lived with her mother and was up for letting her hair down any time. I, again, played the role of the funny, fat friend. They were both pretty, thin, and blonde. So, it was showtime! I got pity beer at parties—you know, given to the fat girl that the beauties are with so you look like you're a nice guy and care about more than getting into their pants. Pity beer tastes just as good... I'm just saying. No regrets..

Fridays were for hangovers and hydrating, so you could stomach going home for the weekend to stock up on groceries and money. I made my rounds to my grandma's, aunt's, and brother's house too. (Maybe it does take a village.) I missed my dad while I was gone during the week. He was in bad health, and I worried about him because I was doing my best to take care of him. My dad did what he wanted and was hard headed. (This seems to be a family trait.) At one point, my taking care of him meant just do my best to keep him out of the hospital. He'd had strokes and was a brittle diabetic that you couldn't make understand that he was *not* following a diabetic diet because he drank Diet Pepsi. My first semester being gone, his A1C was 14. (Normal is under 7.) I had several moments where I almost gave up and went back home. Dad would get mad and say, "I'd do it, and you'd just be here watching me do it. Nothing's gonna change if you come back home. I'll just do it right in front of you, and you'll be wasting money." He really was proud of me. It felt good but added a lot of pressure. I know that my mom was proud of me in her own way. She'd tell everyone that I was following in her footsteps. It wasn't so much that I was; it was just all I ever knew. I really want to go into cosmetology (surprise) and still hope to do that. The problem is, with my health, it's vital that I have health insurance, and carrying my own policy since I've had big surgeries and have a complicated health condition is so expensive, I won't make enough to live on after that bill is paid for.

Don't get me wrong; I'm a decent nurse, but there are so many shady things that happen in healthcare nowadays. Staffing ratios are awful… dishonest healthcare workers, and lack of proper medical supplies, just to name a few. But, when it's all you've done for 17 years and you are alone, a job change would be super difficult. I can't think of anything I could do and make the amount of money that I make now—and again, the insurance.

I've lost several jobs due to my health, but I feel like if I give into disability, I'll lose it altogether. I know the time will come for it, but not now. I think I'll know. So the game is to try to find a job as a nurse that doesn't kill your body. Up to now, it has been night shift mostly, but honestly, after 35, your body just changes. You can't sleep during the day any more and taking energy tabs with your energy drinks works well…until you crash. Let's not forget the palpitations and blood sugar tanking. So you look for a clinic job or something that doesn't kill you that you can do during the day. Then, you are on life sustaining meds and opioids to make your shifts. To date, I've had five brain surgeries. Thank God for good friends and some family members. I'm not sure how I'd have survived this far without them. Being alone doesn't bother me for the most part, but when your health is compromised, it's always in the back of your mind.

OK, back to the nursing school struggle. As I mentioned before, I had made a couple of friends in the program. Both lived locally, so they didn't have to go home every weekend. On weekends when I had hard tests, my parents would send me money, and I'd stay in town. My childhood friend, Kayla, went to the university and would bring stuff if she had happened to go home. Her parents were divorced, and she'd try to sneak into her dad's and bring home elk meat and stuff we could use. She was super busy, trying to take as many classes as she could because she was on a timeline as to how long her dad had to pay for school. She worked her ass off and made great grades. All of this while being in a sorority too. I was doing half as much and would just shake my head wondering how in the hell she was so smart, and I was so dumb. She was like that in high school too, taking all the AP classes. I took Honors English and Honors biology, but I'm pretty sure my homeschool teacher took it easy on me, considering I was sick as hell and could only see light and shadow for five months.

Making friends was usually easy for me. The girls at school liked going out every weekend, and on weekends that I got to stay in town, the funny, fat friend would tag along. I was introduced to their friends. All were great... mostly drunk, but great. It was nice to be with new people. I come from a tiny town with no diversity, and no one even locks their doors. Even to this day, I'm pretty sure it's still that way. I honestly thought that everyone was honest like that. So when Joey wanted to bring DVD's and pizza over, I didn't think anything about it. Remember, people have always been good for the most part in my life. That's what happens when you're from a two-stoplight town; you trust and think everyone is that way. How bad could he be? Laney knew him. A friend of a friend. He was funny in group activities, and if you can make me laugh, you've already won half the battle. I didn't get looked at by most guys back then. That's not a "feel sorry for me" statement; it's just the truth. In that matter, I was socially awkward. I'd not really been on dates. I'd only had one boyfriend, the class clown in high school, who later turned out to love drugs more than he loved laughing. That was really my only experience. Ben sheltered me, and so had the little Mayberry town that I had lived in all my life. Tiny towns were good at covering up family drama. I know most adults in my life knew what our family life was like, but out of respect for some members (my grandma especially), everyone just swept it under the rug. You could run a stop sign, and your dad knew it before you got home.

I also was really close to a guy my senior year, and we went together a couple of years of community college. Feelings got tangled up, and there was sex, but I was the dirty little secret. It was a real learning experience as to what not to do or let happen in the future. Almost 20 years, and it still stings. Things worked out for him. He graduated, got married, and has a baby. I'm happy for him, but I rarely speak to him, and if so, only on social media. I digress…

Joey came over with pizza and a DVD just like he said he would. We sat down on the floor and ate pizza and watched the movie. I can't even remember what it was. I know it was a comedy. After the dvd, the news came on, which meant it was 10 p.m. I was kind of tired, and I needed to do laundry; I wasn't a fan of him watching me fold my underwear anyway. I wasn't sure what to do because he seemed pretty interested in the news, so I just sat back down. After I sat back down, I figured I'd just wait him out. Again, this was pretty new territory. I was the funny fat one that third-wheeled with her pretty friends. My high school boyfriend always left when he was supposed to because my dad and Ben were there, so there was no waiting out anything. Ben would just say, "Time to go," and he would leave. This growing up thing wasn't what I thought it'd be like.

    His mood started changing, and I was a little concerned. Maybe more than a little concerned. I worked on steadying my breath and not showing fear. I remember he turned the TV off and was acting really weird. So I said, "Well, I'm getting tired and have a test tomorrow. (I didn't.) So, we'll have to do this again, but I need to go to bed." He looked at me, almost like he was mad or had just accepted the challenge that I didn't know I'd thrown down. I was completely out of my comfort zone.

Back home, guys would have just left. There are times in your life when you know something bad is going to happen, and you know that there's nothing you can do about it. My dad's gun that he had sent with me was in the closet, and he was standing in front of it. He was a big guy. I knew what was going to happen. I remember thinking at that moment that I was going to get raped. You can be trained to do all the things, but until you're put in that situation, you can't say what you'd do. I'd been trained on this. Our high school had even offered self-defense. One of our wrestling coaches was a black belt in karate, and he showed us so many things. Blank. I could remember nothing. I could either fight and possibly get hurt (my psych nursing said he was psychotic at that moment) or just try to get through it.

In life, you have a fight or flight mode when things like this happen. I remember thinking if my dad or Ben found me, I wanted for them to know that I fought. I was also aware that if I got hit in the head at a certain spot, he could kill me. When he turned on me, things happened so fast, but then again, it lasted forever. He was rough. And not just rough, there were times during this when I thought and hoped that I'd die. I kicked him as hard as I could, and that's when he used his pocket knife to rape me. Literal razor blades inside me. I knew I was bleeding, but kept telling myself it wasn't as bad as it looked or felt. "Now you're wet," he growled, strangling me, and then raped me for what seemed like forever.

I remember thinking, "I'm a statistic now." Once he was finally done, he came inside me and said that he had, "fucked me up too much to get pregnant anyways."

Afterwards, he got dressed and took time to take his dvd out of the player, took the rest of the pizza, and left. As he was leaving, he turned around and looked at me. I was curled up in a ball, trying not to bleed a lot. I only had one pair of sheets. He took the time to tell me to "be good" and locked the door when he left. I wanted a mom at that moment. I knew mine wouldn't deal with this, but at that minute before I got up, I thought if Hannah and I were still close that Julia would have been my mom. But, we had drifted apart, and I didn't even have her number anymore. There was a moment that the child-like feeling had come back. I allowed it to wash over me, then I shook it away. Any child I had in me had died just a few minutes prior. So, like I'd done all my life, I got up.

What happened after that, I can't make sense of. I later learned I reacted the way I did because I was just trying to deal with the trauma. I got up. I put my sheets in my washer with bleach. I remember being sad because they had little flowers on them that I knew would fade with the bleach, and I'd bought those sheets because they matched my bedding. I poured peroxide over the blood that was on my comforter like it was the normal thing to do. At this point it was 2:00 a.m. I called my brother. He was working the night shift in a glass mill. He picked up right away and wanted to know what was wrong. I couldn't tell him. I couldn't say the words. Finally, he asked me if I'd been raped after going through a million questions as he tried to figure out why I was up so late and why I was sobbing. I told him yes, and the line got quiet. I immediately felt guilty that I had told him because of how he must've felt. Just working his shift, minding his own business, and then having that bomb dropped on him. I could tell he was trying to hold his shit together, and he didn't know what to say or do. That's when I realized how big this was: Ben had no words. I had shocked him so much he didn't have any words. So I told him not to come and I was fine, and I just wanted to let somebody know. I knew he didn't need to miss work and telling my dad might actually kill him; somehow if I had told my mom in the moment, it would somehow be my fault, and I couldn't deal with that.

So, I did the textbook thing that you're not supposed to do. I took the hottest bath and scrubbed as much as I could. I cleaned under my fingernails. I scrubbed everywhere. I was outside of myself for a little bit. I had pink bath water from the blood and all the scrubbing. I threw away the clothes I was wearing. I think I had to take a three-day break from everything because even the best makeup can't cover up swelling. I looked and felt like I'd been in a bar fight. On the outside, the bruises healed, and I went on auto pilot for the next few months. I went to work; I went to school. My grades weren't great. I did my best to stay numb, but the problem with me going numb is you feel nothing at all. No more feelings of happiness or joy. Even feeling productive after you've finished an assignment is gone. I couldn't process feelings, good or bad. My body was doing weird things that I assumed was its way of reacting to the way I was just trying to survive. I had tried to get counseling, but they put me with a male counselor and as he opened the door, he yelled, "Is this the rape victim?" and I all but climbed up the office wall to get out. The worst thing in my life had just happened, and I was expected to talk to a man who had called me a victim. I instantly decided that I wasn't going to do that; this happens to women every day and they get through it. So I got up and just kept going——kind of.

The stress of trying to keep up the appearance of a "normal" nursing student was hard. I felt like crap all the time and was exhausted because I rarely slept or ate. When I did sleep, I'd wake up screaming from continuously reliving the nightmare. I wanted to get checked out, but knew I'd have to use my dad's insurance to get seen, and I didn't want him to know anything, so I went to the free clinic.

As with any new patient, there comes a shit ton of paperwork. Family history—easy. I had filled out a ton of these when my dad saw a new doctor so I knew this frontwards and backwards. Chief complaint—not so easy. "I feel tired and crappy and think I need a B-12 shot?" Last menstrual period? I have no idea. I can't even tell you when I last showered. So the nurse practitioner did an exam and had me do a urine test. She left the room for what seemed like hours. She finally came back. She walked through the exam room door with a chart in her hands. "Well, I think I know why you feel like crap… You're pregnant." I had put the whole event out of my head so I denied it and demanded that the test be redone. Turns out any positive, they do another test before they show or tell the patient. I kept thinking I couldn't be pregnant because I hadn't had sex since I went to community college. I didn't call what happened sex. I called it evil. So I'm five months pregnant.

I've had no prenatal care; I hadn't done anything since this evil had happened. No drinking or anything. I never smoked. So things went fast with this discovery. Luckily, the universe kept the baby safe. I hadn't really eaten much, and the provider explained that the baby takes what it needs and leaves the mom with whatever is left. Due to the extenuating circumstances, they squeezed me in with an ultrasound for measurements. I measured 21 weeks, which was exactly correct. I was sent home with pamphlets and samples of prenatal vitamins. How in the hell am I going to make this work! I can't go home with this. So I handled this like I'd handled everything since it happened. I ignored it. I took prenatal vitamins faithfully, and tried to eat more. I was due about the first of the year. I'd figure something out until I could finish school. I wasn't going to tell my family until I went home for Christmas. School was getting harder so I didn't go home much anyway. I didn't really look any different at this point. I was regularly a thick girl, so I could pull it off. If I had to go home, they'd just think that I was fatter. Which, if you ask my mother, was expected of me.

So I worked both jobs as much as I could. Ms. D knew, and Lauren and Laney knew. I wasn't close to anyone else in class. Hoodies covered a lot, and no one cared enough to ask. I told Kayla. She asked me what my plan was. I was winging it. My plan was I was going to finish school with a baby. There were programs and daycares that would help single moms, and I'd just figure it out as I go. I saved money as much as I could. I bought a crib and a carseat. I was going to breastfeed. Honestly, not because it was better, but because it was cheaper. I was very smart about what little money I had. At 6 ½ months, I woke up looking pregnant. Not fat. There was a bump that seemed to appear overnight. It was a big kick in the face to know that this was, in fact, happening. Kayla helped a lot. Her dad owned oil wells so she let me help her clean the trailers, which gave me more cash. Any extra time I had, I was in class. I tried to stay as busy as I could and keep my mind on anything else besides what was going on in my body right then.

They say when something is wrong, you have a sense of impending doom. I went to class 28 weeks pregnant. I was abnormally tired…like almost falling asleep driving tired. I stopped at Sonic and got a cherry lime slush on my way home and went to bed. The baby (I had named her Rylee) did this kick and jab thing that she'd never done before. (Later, I was told this was a suspected seizure in utero.) It was hard kicking. You could see my belly jerking around, but I'd just had a cold slush and figured that had pissed her off. I woke up in the middle of the night, knowing that something was really wrong. She hadn't moved since. I called the hospital and was told to come in.

I drove myself. I was trying to make myself numb going in. The nurses were a lot nicer to me as a patient than as a student nurse. I put on a gown and waited for an ultrasound. They gave me a Coke to drink, thinking the caffeine would wake her up. Everyone tried their best to smile and have soft voices to keep me calm, but at that moment it was like my whole body had been bathed in Lidocaine. I knew she was gone. I was just waiting for confirmation. So they do the ultrasound, and I wait and wait to hear her little heartbeat. They even put an attachment that buzzed my belly, basically trying to wake her up. After what felt like hours, there was confirmation that the sweet baby girl would forever be sleeping.

Now comes the part that no one thinks of: there is a dead baby inside of me. My choices were to go home and let nature take its course…this could take days… or they can give me an IV of meds to start labor then. There was no way I was leaving that hospital with a dead baby in my belly, so medication it was. It's funny thinking back; it never occurred to me to call someone to hold my hand. We'd started this alone, we'd finish it alone too. To the woman that has a big baby and the woman that has a preemie…you both had labor and both had babies, and labor is absolutely real. It doesn't matter what size baby you end up having. Labor was awful, but I begged every time a nurse came in to turn up the IV. I just needed to be done with this. It took hours, and those were the longest hours of my life to date. Rylee was the only baby that I ever had. She was born forever sleeping, and thank God, she looked like me. The nurses cleaned her and swaddled her. They gave me all the time I needed. She just looked like she was sleeping. Tiny and sleeping. She even had what looked to be strawberry hair coming in. I held her for two hours. I really didn't believe in God anymore, but I had her baptized, just in case I was wrong. She shouldn't have to pay for a belief I have, so I felt like it covered her either way.

The rest of the night/morning was a bit blurry. I went to my car (left AMA) and called Kayla. I just asked her to bring a friend to drive my car. Luckily she had roommates because it never occurred to me who she'd have found. I remember it was dark out. She came right away. I didn't have to say much. She knew. I stayed at her house the first night just because I wasn't sure what was normal and what wasn't. I left the hospital with a shoebox instead of a baby. A preemie diaper, a booty, a bracelet with her name, and a pic of her and a pic of me holding her.

That was the start of my breakdown. I tried to keep going. Left foot, right foot, repeat. It was increasingly hard to stay numb. I couldn't keep up with everything in my life. I took a twelve-week leave of absence from school to try to get my head straight. I was failing at that point anyway. Nothing made sense when my world was crashing down. I told my mom about the rape, but not Rylee. I felt the need to protect my dead baby from her, and I didn't tell my dad because he wanted a grandbaby so bad, he wouldn't have cared how she made it into the world. I've told a few people in my life, but not many. Not that I feel like she's a dirty little secret, but I just feel the need to protect her from nosy people and questions. I felt like I'd answered enough at the time.

It took me 20 years and many mental health problems snowballing to get me to see a psychiatrist and get help. It cost me relationships. It helped cost me a marriage. It's something that I work on constantly to keep the relationship that I have stable. My now boyfriend knows, and we work on it. It does get better, but it's always there. I have a hard time on her birthday. I get jealous of pregnant people. (It's a continuous work in progress.) I'm happy for my friends that have babies, but I'll always feel that I have an unfinished life since I don't have any children. I've had several pregnancies since, but none to term.

I keep a fur baby at all times, but that's no substitute for my forever sleeping baby.

I'd basically given up on the idea of being a nurse. I stayed home for a while, but I went back to finish out my lease since it was something that had to be paid for anyway. Besides, it gave me some space away from people. I was a functional zombie. I'd been put on some mental health meds: one that helped me stop waking up, screaming from nightmares, and another that was an antidepressant. I'd sent Ms. D an email telling her that I didn't think I was going back to school, and that I appreciated everything she had done for me, and that I'd never forget the way she carried herself, and the way she fought for me during the program.

On the last day of my leave from school (I was being dropped the next day), Ms. D showed up at my apartment. Her SUV was still running, and she let herself in as soon as I opened the door. Stepping into my kitchen, she looked me up and down. I hadn't brushed my hair in days, let alone showered. I must've been a hot mess.
 "Put your shoes on and brush your teeth; you're going to class tonight." She wasn't messing around and wasn't taking any excuses. She knew that I had no intention of going back. I just didn't think it was in me. My future plans went as far as the next mind-numbing TV show that played. I didn't really care. Mental health meds are great, but they aren't magic wands that make your life great just by taking them. It takes work, and I didn't have the energy. I didn't care about anything anymore.

She put her purse on my bar and held both of my hands and looked me right in the eyes, which made me incredibly nervous. Any type of intimacy from anyone made me want to peel my skin off at that point.

"Look at me," she said in her 'I'm not fucking around' voice that had a little bit of Ireland in it. "Today is your last day to be in the program. If I take roll tonight, and you aren't there, that's it. You're out of the program. It would give the admin. so much satisfaction to fail one of my misfits. Go brush your teeth and hair, put a bra on, and I'll find your shoes. You don't have to do a damn thing but take up a chair, but you're going. If you don't, *HE* wins. Everything was for nothing. Now, where's your backpack?"

I just looked at her. Why was she taking this time? Why wasn't she leaving me alone like the rest of the instructors and students? I didn't know what to say or do, so I just sat there with my head down, staring at the leather of her purse, sitting on the bar. "You need to throw some dry shampoo and deodorant on because you stink, but we'll worry about that after class." That's the thing about Ms. D; it never occurs to you to tell her 'no.' "Go brush your teeth, spray your hair, and wash your face. Deodorant. We'll call it good. I'll start looking for your stuff."

I fumbled toward my teeny bathroom. I hadn't shut the bathroom door since everything happened, so I stood there with my hand on the door knob. She knew. Ms. D always knew.

"I've been a nurse for over 30 years, and nothing has ever shocked me or impressed me. You can leave the door open." While I fumbled with my toothbrush, she went through my apartment, found my old backpack, and threw some books in it. "Ok, put on your shoes; let's get moving."

I didn't say much on the ride to school. It felt like it took forever, but it was just right outside of town. I don't know if she had told the evening class what she was doing, but I was so thankful that no one reacted or really even acknowledged me that day. Ms. D stuck to her word. I sat in the corner in the back with my book open, and I did nothing. We got an evening meal break and going down to the cafeteria sounded like torture. It was always loud with laughter, and I didn't really engage with people anymore. So as everyone left for dinner, I started to panic. Ms. D left for a few minutes but returned with two lunches. She opened my can of Dr. Pepper. There was a sandwich and chips in a paper bag. She went back to her desk and ate the same lunch she gave me. Thinking back, I don't think I ate anything. I moved things around because I knew Ms. D had the forethought to bring me food. The truth was, I really hadn't eaten much for months. I'd lost weight, even though I was still big. My clothes didn't fit, and I was just out of sorts in general. Luckily, my parents mailed in my rent and paid bills after they found out about the rape. They generally had left me alone. I think it was mostly because no one knew what to say or do, and mailing my bills in for me was just something that I didn't have to do or think about. The one time I did put effort into going home, I'd walked by my mom's room and heard her telling someone on the phone, "We'd just been through a rape." *We* hadn't been through anything. *Me. Just me.* Then Rylee. *We* hadn't been through shit. At that point, it was decided that I had "permission" to go back to my apartment until the lease was up. Then I had to come home. Mom constantly reminded me how much everything cost. I felt guilty enough so that didn't help.

The class took forever, and I scribbled in my notebook for hours. Finally, the other students started closing books and left one by one. After the last student left, Ms. D gathered her stuff and just quietly said, "C'mon, let's go." I laid my head on the side of the window so the air could hit me and closed my eyes. I felt so old. My body was now old. Surgery didn't make my body old. Countless spinal taps didn't make my body old. Living without my forever sleeping baby had killed my body and wrecked my soul. I lived with the added guilt that the whole time I was pregnant with Rylee, I thought of her as something I was going to have to deal with. I didn't realize that I'd made a bond with the little person that was making me feel like crap and turning my world upside down. Life wasn't supposed to feel like this in my early twenties. You weren't supposed to pray that the universe takes you out this young. Waking up should be something to be thankful for, not realize that you're alive and get mad that you had to do another day of this.

I would often think of suicide. I had several plans. The main one was me driving off a bridge right outside of town as fast as I could. It got to the point where I couldn't even go to that side of town the few times that I did have to get out because I'd find myself heading towards the bridge. If it hadn't been for the thought of my brother and dad grieving for the loss of a little sister and daughter, I'd have done it in a second.

That's the part of suicide that always stopped me. The selfish part. Yeah, I'd no longer feel pain in my body and mind, but then my dad has to lose a daughter just like I did, and I couldn't do that to him. My brother would blame himself somehow, thinking he could've done something or said something. He'd carry that with him for the rest of his life, and I couldn't do that to him—not when he was my saving grace growing up. I wouldn't pay him back that way. Instead, I walked around like a zombie and just existed. I wanted to be a zombie. Zombies didn't cry every night. I never went home. I was looked at too much, when all I wanted to do was blend in. When you're a chubby redhead, you're gonna stick out, regardless. Especially in a small town. So when I did have to go home, I made a beeline for my bedroom and just prayed that my mom didn't start hollering at me to go do something that she could damn well do herself…like get up, go all the way across the house, and get her a Dr. Pepper.

We finally rolled up to my apartment. "Well, thanks." I had my hand on the door and would have tucked and rolled from the vehicle, which was still moving at this point.
"No, I'm coming in too." (I was in the evening program which ended at 10 p.m. By this time, it was almost 10:45.)
"Please Ms. D…I've had enough for one day." Hell, a week or a month. "I don't understand; I went to class like you wanted. What now?" She stared through my soul. This was a Ms. D thing. I've never met a human before or since that can do it like her.
"I let you get away with coming to class a mess today because Admin. thought that they had your ass. Now, we go in. We clean up, we wash your sheets, and you're taking a shower. You always came to class so put together: makeup done, nails, everything. We're doing that again. *This*"—she waved her hand from my head to my toes—"stops tonight. Tonight, Lou gets her power back. I'll pick you up every day if I need to, and slowly you'll start focusing on the curriculum, and you're gonna graduate, and you're going to thrive." The thought of doing this every day made me want to drive nails down my arms. I honestly didn't think that it was in me to do this five days a week.

"Can I ask you a question?" I'd given in and rested my head on the window.
"Yes, but you have to look at me when you do it." Eye contact was a true struggle. I turned in the seat to where our green eyes met. "Why do you care? You have had so many students come and go; what's one more student that slipped through the cracks?"

She looked at her steering wheel and took a deep breath. Now it was her turn to keep it together, I guess. When she looked back, her watery green eyes were fiery. "Because one day, you're gonna have a patient that is going through hell, and you're going to be able to relate to them. This is changing you, but it's going to make you a great nurse. Life changes us. Events change us. But we have the power to change it for the better. It's ok to be sad. It's ok to be pissed off—God knows I am! We just can't let you fail. If you fail, you're letting him win. It's ok to need help right now, too. So c'mon… Let's go get this stuff done."

We went into the apartment, and she immediately went into work mode. Sorting laundry, "Is this dirty or clean?" she asked. I was just honest.
"I don't know." I had a stackable washer/dryer unit in my apartment, but I rarely changed clothes, so I just didn't see the point in washing clothes. I didn't see the point in a lot of things.
"Okay, we can wash your scrubs and the stuff that you need for school, and we'll deal with the rest tomorrow." I went into my walk-in closet and pulled out some pj bottoms and a t-shirt that said something cute about being a nursing student. I shut the door, which was a victory of itself. It was the first time that I took a good look at myself, a really good look at myself. I had lost weight… it was a hell of a way to do it though. I had refused to look at myself in the mirror naked until then. I knew that I had internal scars from the knife but didn't realize that the outside of my vagina and thighs looked like a cutting board. I drew in a deep breath. Stretch marks from my sleeping girl were on my sides and stomach. I knew those were there. I was pretty protective of them. She and I had made them together, and it was one of the few things that I had of her that was permanent. I had decided to donate my breast milk. My

milk had come in almost immediately, and one of the nurses had commented how there were sick babies in the NICU that could use it. So I pumped and froze and brought it in weekly. So I had heavy milk gravity going on.

"I don't hear any water running in there!" Ms. D chimed. I quickly turned the water on like a little kid who was going to get in trouble, and the shower came on. I put it on the hottest I could stand. My hair was so dirty that the first try, the shampoo wouldn't even suds. Three shampoos and a conditioning treatment later, it was almost normal. Now to shave my legs; I hadn't done that in ages. I got that taken care of and used my antibacterial body wash and shaved my underarms. I washed my face last. (I know, not in the right order, but neither was I.) I remember thinking that Julia would have some magic mask that would make my skin soft again. I missed Hannah and her. They had moved back to Alaska when we were in middle school, and I was destroyed. My sanctuary moved thousands of miles away. I thought about them often. That random thought calmed me enough to open the bathroom door. There was no telling what was on the other side.

To my surprise, my place was clean, for the most part. Ms. D had ordered a pizza and had taken a piece. "Do you feel better?" she asked.
"I feel cleaner," I said.
"Ok, well, I'm going home now. Your scrubs are in the dryer so when they buzz, hang them up so they won't wrinkle." I promised, and off my red-headed fairy godmother went. I put the pizza in the fridge; once the dryer was done, I did what I was told and hung everything up.

Have you ever been so exhausted that you couldn't sleep? Just breathing and blinking took everything out of me. That was my life. I could take cat naps here and there, but it had been months since I'd slept all night. I'd mostly stared at the empty crib that I refused to take down. It wasn't much. It was a light oak porta-crib; I'd made cream-colored bumper pads and a top blanket with a sewing machine that my grandma had given me. The material was plain and had been a major mark down. All I had to do was buy a couple of fitted sheets. I had bought the letters of her name and used the same cream-colored ribbon to hang them above her bed. My place was super tiny, but I'd made sure she'd have a good sized corner of it. I'd wonder if she'd be up right now fussing because she was hungry or needed a diaper change. I kept the app on my phone to see what her milestones would be. I did things like that at night when I couldn't sleep. I'd take Benadryl, but it didn't help. My face was starting to sink in, and I had really dark circles under my eyes. My face had developed texture since I no longer took care of it. I had the good makeup to cover it up; I just didn't have the desire to. As far as I was concerned, I wasn't going to be looked at again, so what did it matter? I used to stay up too late watching YouTube videos about how to apply makeup. Remember…Momzilla didn't wear makeup.

No one taught me, like everything else in my life so far; I just figured it out.

Now I watched music videos—you know the kind where the lyrics speak to you? I have always found peace in music, even then. I journaled, but ended up ripping it to pieces because I didn't want anyone to know what was in my head. It's taken almost 17 years for me to even put it down in writing. Nights lasted forever, and I dreaded them before the sun would even start going down.

Eventually, the sun came up, and that was what gave me permission to get out of bed and try to stay busy. Autopilot only works when there are things of importance to do. I didn't really have friends anymore, because I didn't know how to act around people. Kayla would come by sometimes when she could and act like nothing had happened. I appreciated that. The fact was that what had happened happened, and nothing that anyone said was going to change that. I've never been a person comforted by words. She never pushed, but let me do my thing. She'd try to get me out of the apartment. Sometimes, I would give in knowing that she was so busy trying to fight the time clock on her parents' divorce agreement that I knew she had moved her schedule around just to come by. We'd go eat sometimes; I had a favorite Italian restaurant, and we'd go to it. Food just wasn't appealing anymore. But, she was one of the few who put effort into being my friend. It might have gone unnoticed then, but looking back, I know she cared. We didn't have to talk or anything. Sometimes, in her not so subtle way, she'd tell me that I was letting myself go again by bringing her wax kit over and doing my eyebrows, bringing polish over and painting my toes, or she'd nonchalantly stop by the Bath and Body Works sale and bring over body wash and lotion. I knew I was a mess; I just didn't care. She was one of those friends who'd walk in, put a load of laundry in the washer, throw something in the crockpot, and try to pick up some of my chaos.

I was at class every evening. I'd even gotten to the point where I would drive myself. I still sat in the corner. Lauren and Laney didn't know how to act at first, so they would just sit far away from me and smile when I'd look up to see one of them looking at me. Finally, I guess Ms. D had had enough of it, and when we were all studying, (the girls in the front, me as close to the door as I could get), "Alright, this is enough," she said to no one in particular. Then she looked at Lauren and Laney and said, "She's not made of porcelain; if that were true, she'd have broken months ago. Lou, get your stuff and come up here before I lock you in a closet and tell Jesus you died!" This was Ms. D's loving way to tell the girls it was time for some normalcy in the classroom. She would let us work together in the classroom, and I had missed that. I needed to hear things out loud. I could read it ten times, and it would never soak in, but if we talked about it, it clicked. I didn't realize how lonely I had been in class. The "class clown" had been dead for months, and I'm sure I wasn't approachable. I was holding up my end of the bargain, (rather, demand) that I would take up a chair during class time hours, and Ms. D would figure out a way not to fail me and also give admin. the middle finger while smiling. I don't know how she did it, because I had no productivity for a long time. Slowly, however, I started turning in work instead of near empty sheets of paper that just said, "I'm sorry, Ms. D." I was still behind, but instead of going home and crying all night… There were still tears. Every. Night. I started using the time that I dreaded between sun-down and sun-up to try to do homework. I would leave the questions which I had no clue about and couldn't find in the book for when I got to class. Ms. D would help me with those; she'd make me understand. I was slowly seeing light at the end of the tunnel. I just wasn't sure if it was sunlight or an oncoming train. Either way, I kept going.

I went to school one day, and everyone that saw me would smile. This made me really suspicious and nervous. I wanted to go back out to my car and go back home. Even though I sat with the girls, I was completely fine with trying to be a wallflower. When Ms. D came in, she looked at me, dramatically put her books down on her desk, and said, "Finally! The girl wears mascara!" When I got up that morning, I'd unknowingly fallen back into part of an old routine. Cheap coffee, sugary creamer, and makeup. It wasn't anything spectacular, but I had blush, lip gloss, and mascara on. Lauren and Laney giggled, and Ms. D winked at me. I closed my eyes and took a deep breath. Slowly, I was coming back. At a snail's pace, but progress is progress. I was getting used to eye contact and would even sometimes go to the cafeteria. Ms. D always stayed in the classroom and acted busy grading papers, but I knew it was for those panic attacks when the giggling and loud talking and just too many people around sent me all but running down the hallway back to the classroom.

I'd learned that a person can live off way less food that I had once thought. I ate something when I got home most of the time, but that was pretty much it. I became the queen of crockpot, although sometimes I had major failures. My idea was just to put random shit in there, and it'd be cooked when I got home. My dad had started coming around, and when he did, he always brought good meats that were "Lou" friendly. He cut everything up and made it into single servings. He'd bring can goods, fresh tomatoes, and cucumbers out of his garden. Even though he was disabled, he'd find a way to garden. He planted everything into big buckets, and they tasted just as good without the danger of him falling in the yard. I was sure to make a big deal over those, which I truly loved and ate first. He'd always give me money, although sometimes it was a ten-dollar bill, depending on what part of the month he came over. I'd tell him I was fine, but being the bull-headed guy that he was, I ended up taking it. He would have given me his last dollar and not given it a second thought. Looking back now, it was a pride thing. He didn't care if that was the only $10 that he had. He was resourceful and would get by. He always wanted me to have enough gas money to get back home if I ever decided I needed to. If I had refused it, it would have hurt his heart. I don't think I'd ever done that on purpose in my adulthood, though I used to get mad at him for being gone so much when we were kids. Ben and I really lived through some rough times, and for the most part, he was only there when he was sleeping or watching his evening TV shows at night. I used to beg my dad to divorce my mom, but he knew how much more money she made and that she would take us, just to hurt him She reminded him quite often how much money she made vs. how much he didn't, which I will still say, to this day, drove him right to the casino. I'm not excusing it—Dad had never been a saint and messed up big, but she never let him forget it.

At this point, Ben was working at a glass shop and was doing pretty well. He worked nights so that did well for me since on his days off he'd try to keep the same schedule, and sometimes he'd come over. He'd buy late night pizza, or we'd go to a breakfast place. I can't remember the real name of it, but locals called it "The Greasy Spoon." It was open all night so we ate and then would just watch as the drunks came in to sober up after the last call at all the bars. Most of the time, he'd take me to Walmart. I was thankful for a few reasons. The store was mostly empty with night time stockers, so I tended to panic less. The other was because I got to really take my time and look at things. He never said a word; he just stuck by me even when I knew he'd rather be looking at hunting supplies and not looking for new scrubs and underwear that weren't way too big and were at risk of falling off. He's never been embarrassed by things like that. He'd go get me tampons while he was in high school. Most guys would've run. To him, it was just something that I needed, so he got it. He'd let me fill the cart up and add a few things that he thought I needed too, paid for it all, and then helped me put it away or put it together for me, depending on what the big purchase of the month was. "You know Dad's really proud of you, right?" Which was also his way of saying that he was too.

Ben should've gotten to go to school too. He had a plan to go to some sort of tech school in Texas after his senior year, but mom shit all over that dream. There just wasn't enough money, he wouldn't make it, he was going down there to party, etc. There was a point after he'd filled out his FAFSA that he just kinda gave up. Something she said was the final end of his dream. She squashed it. When I first started going to school, I was afraid that he would resent me, but nothing but encouragement came from him. He did end up going to a nearby tech school and got brake certified, but he started doing hard manual work as soon as he graduated high school.

Ben worked hard and played hard. Both he and his wife (still pisses me off to say it) had four-wheelers and would load them up along with some friends and take them to a place called "Little Sahara." I was too much of a wimp, along with my doctor's voice in my head, "Do you like brain surgery?" At this point, I'm surprised I didn't walk around with a helmet. Brain surgery is no joke, people. Protect your noggin. You only get one, and there's only so much they can do to fix it.

Ben and Avery seemed to be doing ok. He'd always tell me I was welcome there any time. Avery agreed, but we both knew she didn't really mean it. She mainly just went along with whatever Ben said. I would housesit for them when they did stuff like go to concerts. He lived on the lake, and it was peaceful. He had an alarm system that could lock you up as tight as Fort Knox, so that was nice, and he had a big, goofy dog named Cheyenne, that I was certain would fuck somebody up if they got through. They always left a fridge full of food and money for pizza if I wanted it. There was a gas station a couple of miles down the road that made pizza and what I call "Trucker Food"—chicken strips, potato wedges, and pop.

It's funny really. I'd gotten so used to my little apartment at that point; I was never scared to be alone there. I had accepted the fact that I would live alone until the disease process messed with my brain to the point that I started forgetting things and would not be balanced enough to be on my own. Ben always swore (and still does to this day) that I had a place with him wherever he was when that happened. We had a deal: if it got too much for him to care of me then he would find some morphine and kill me. I would have anaphylaxis if I had it, so it wouldn't take much. I think he'd do it. We'd talked about it several times while learning about this brain thing. I didn't want to be put in a nursing home in my fifties. I grew up in one with my mom being a Director of Nurses in one for most of my life. If I can't take care of myself and require that much care, then put me in the ground somehow. I've had a DNR since I was 18. I have every faith in him that he'll do what needs to be done when it needs to be done. Kind of dark thinking, but no one should have to live with the progression of a disease. We can put dogs to sleep when they get sick. Why can't we do this for our loved ones?

So, on the outside, it looked like Ben and Avery were doing really well, but they weren't. Ben texted me about 3:00 a.m. one night to tell me that they were splitting up. (See what I did in the first part of the book: "I was here before you, and I'll be here after you.") Not that I wanted my brother's heart to break, but she was beneath him. I don't say that as a little sister; I say that as a realist. I never asked for details, but you gotta love the small town gossip. She had been cheating; I'm sure he wasn't innocent in all of it. I know that he kept the house for a little while and then moved to an apartment in Tulsa to be closer to work.

School was getting easier to focus on. As long as I stayed busy and exhausted myself on the daily, I didn't think of the chaos that was my life. I still rarely came home unless Ben asked me to. Dad would usually come and take me to dinner every once and awhile. Mom basically called to make sure I was up on my school work, because how would it look if the "SuperNurse's" daughter were to fail? I think this is why I don't like talking on the phone. The only one that I actually talk to on the phone is my now boyfriend, and I will do that. I guess that's a positive. It only took close to 20 years. I'm not sure who in my little town knew about the rape, but with gossip being a big focus of entertainment, I did my best to stay outta there.

I had finally finished the curriculum, and it was my last clinical night. There was a tradition that Ms. D had: we all went to Braums to get ice cream to celebrate. It was the first time that I hadn't dreaded going out in a crowd of people in a long time. I'd been to hell and back to finish that program, and I deserved to take a deep breath—and even eat some peppermint ice cream. I took a picture with Ms. D, and I still have it hanging up in my home. I was closer to the end of the tunnel, but the state boards were next, and that's what really counted.

In my life, I've failed every major test I've taken the first time. I failed my written driver's test; I failed my actual driving test. I just don't test well it seems. It was $200 to take the boards, so I'd saved up $400 because I expected to fail it the first time, just like everything else. I told very few people the date of my test. I graduated in August, and I couldn't get a date until October. I used that time to really study. I wanted to stay in the town that I went to school in, but the rate of pay was low because it was a college town. I had decided to move to Tulsa, which was a bigger town than the town I went to school in. I was nervous, but had gained so much life experience that I thought I could do it. It was only a half hour from my tiny town so I could come home if I got homesick for my dad or brother, and it was easier to meet halfway.

The day of the test, Kayla took me because it was in Oklahoma City, and I was not familiar with the city. Kayla seemed to be familiar with everything. You just needed to give her an address or some half-ass directions, and we'd end up there. I think that was from cleaning all those trailers on her dad's oil rigs. We'd end up in the weirdest spots. She waited while I took the hardest test I've ever taken. You took the test on the computer, and you couldn't go back and change your answers. It would pick up on a weak spot and just hammer the hell out of you with questions. Everyone in my class that passed had 75 questions. I had 283. I worked hard not to cry and told myself that this was expected, and I would pass it the next time. It was like a rollercoaster that I just wanted off of, and the questions kept coming. Finally, the test ended. I picked up what was left of my confidence and went to the locker assigned to me to get my purse. Kayla knew my face. She just looked at me and said, "You can do it again. Think of it as a practice test." Waiting was awful. You had to wait two days and then go to the site to type in a code, and it told you your future. Of course, by this time I was living with my parents again, and Mom was right behind me as I nervously typed in my code. It took forever for it to connect to everything it was supposed to. (Yes, I lived through dial-up.) I opened my eyes. It had my name and in big green letters it said PASSED! I thought for sure whatever computer that graded my test had a serious virus, but I printed it out along with the page that said my paper license would be in the mail. Mom just smiled. Dad said, "Congratulations, Sissy, you did it!"

After I caught my breath and composed myself, I got my cell phone and went out to the back porch. I had a call to make. "Hello," came from a familiar voice.
 "Ms. D! I passed that dirty bitch!" She laughed, and I cried a little.
 "There was no doubt in my mind that you could do this. Congratulations. You are now my colleague."

Jack and Kathy, who is actually a cousin, for any reason claim me as their daughter. I wasn't allowed to meet any of my dad's family until I was 18 because my mom said they were awful people, and once I was 18, I could do what I wanted to do. I met Jack, Kathy, and their three kids at a Christmas dinner at their house. Walking in, I was home. It was so nice to have family in Tulsa, especially when you're new to the town. I remember I met Cate when she was about five. She was cute and knew it. Kathy had taught her early to stand up for herself. She kind of had to. She was the baby and 18 years younger than the oldest son: the biggest surprise of Jack and Kathy's life. I was still guarded and had no intention of falling in love with this little girl. Cate had other plans. I can tell you the exact minute it happened. Kathy had invited me to lunch with her and Cate at a Mexican restaurant. As we started to cross the street, Cate grabbed my hand to hold it. It took me off guard because we didn't really touch in my family. I must've jerked away a little because she just grinned and said, "Well, I can't cross the street without holding an adult's hand, silly!"

Jack made sure my car was up and running, and Kathy sent me home with food every time I came out to see them. Feeding you was her love language. To this day, I'm still angry at my mother for making me wait until I was 18 to find this family. I had missed out on so much. I needed Kathy when I was Cate's age.

It took me a few months to get this "grown-up job" thing down. I had a duplex that was really cute and older like I like. Kathy helped me find a safe spot that I could afford. I was working in an internal medicine clinic at the university, and I had several third and fourth year residents that I took care of. (Yes, I said take care of.) They had some of the busiest schedules that I'd ever seen. So I'd do extra stuff for them like pull labs that were questionable, fill out prior authorizations for medications... that I was good at. If I couldn't get it approved, it just didn't happen. I'd comb through charts for dates that other meds were tried and failed. My residents knew they just had to sign the paper, and it would be done. Some of those residents I still stay in touch with. One, I consider my best friend and text her on the daily even now, almost 20 years later.

I got married. Ms. D came to my bridal shower—with a crockpot. I introduced her as the reason that I was a nurse. Most just smiled, but few truly understood that she was. Kayla was there and sat next to me, writing down gifts and who had gotten me what. We took a really great picture that day. I still have that one too.

My dad was diagnosed with multiple myeloma, and my world stopped. My life was about him and nothing else: eight months from diagnosis to death. He declined chemo. He just had too many other health issues. His body couldn't take it, and he wanted to enjoy what time he had left. We elected a hospice so he could die with dignity. My brother had had a redheaded baby girl that we found out about when she was about six months old. She was Dad's reason for getting up every day until he couldn't. At his funeral, she was about 18 months old. I held her because I needed to hold something, or I was going to crumble. She was a busy little thing that wriggled out of my lap. Her mom jumped up to get her, and I said, "No, PaPa said it was okay," so she went where she pleased during his service. That little girl had no rules when my dad was around. It was kind of fitting that she'd tear it up at his funeral. So we let her. The man I call my stand-in dad spoke at his funeral. He was the one that had promised to take care of me, so he could finally let go. We had all given him permission, but he kept hanging on. I couldn't figure out why he wouldn't just let go. Jack came in with a guitar and softly played music and let him know that I was his daughter from now on. He'd watch out for me. Dad died about twenty minutes later. Jack has always kept his word. There's never been a time that I thought I couldn't call him.

I think my now ex-husband hung around for maybe a week. I'll put most of the blame on myself. I didn't have it in me to work on our relationship at the time. I had just given one hundred percent of myself to a disease that killed my father. My SuperMan had just died, and I didn't really care to do anything but lie in bed and cry for him. Tim just wasn't going to stick around for it. We'd been through countless miscarriages: he traveled all over for work so he was used to being on his own and having a wife that was functional when he got home. I signed a piece of paper, and it was like our marriage had never happened. I was so numb at that point, I don't think I even grieved for our failed relationship. He had an apartment and everything he needed by the end of the week. Looking back, he knew that once my dad died, he was leaving and began to carve out a plan. I can't even tell you where he is today.

After ten years, I can tell you that I don't think I ever loved him in the way that you should love someone you marry. It just made sense to marry him: he was crazy about me, and I thought I was always going to be numb. It was the logical thing to do. I didn't have to work full time, and he carried the medical insurance on me. Life was easier with two people, so when he asked me to marry him, I said yes. I'm not saying that I had no feelings for him…I did. I just loved him more like a best friend. I didn't think I was ever going to be more than numb, and I could go along with it. At first, we were really good about trying to do married stuff, but in the end, we both gave up. I'm sorry that I went along with it and hope that he moved on without too many glitches. He couldn't handle seeing my dad sick, and I still hold a grudge against him not going to see my dad when he would specifically ask for him. I would have to make up excuses that he was out of town, when in fact, he was at home sitting on the couch, hiding from the reality of cancer. I don't think I could have gotten over that, even with couples therapy. I saw that as weakness, and I just have never had room for weak men in my life.

It's cruel how life continues when someone you love dies. Bills have to be paid. You have to get up and go to work. You still have to go to the grocery store. Pets still have to be fed. You have to remember to eat sometimes too. You live in the past: the part of the world where your dad wasn't in the ground, decaying. At the same time, you have to move forward. That's the best way to explain the death of a loved one.

At first, anything and everything that you do has a memory connected to them. Then one day, you've gone a whole morning without thinking of him. You feel awful, because you feel like he's worth being remembered all the time. It's been ten years since I held his hand while he let go of life. That was the deal. I promised Dad that I would hold his hand while he died. I held his hand for hours to make sure I made good on that promise. It shattered me.

Sometimes I can go a whole day without thinking of him. Sometimes I can go longer. He's always on the tip of my tongue though. I have pictures up on my walls that make me think of him. He deserves to be remembered, but he wouldn't want me living in the past either. So, with time, you figure out how to live without him, but do things that would make him proud of you. Sometimes, something Dad used to say comes right out of my mouth, and I just have to look up at the universe and know that it was from him. My brother named his youngest after him. I'm glad he did; my dad would have been so proud of Ben. His middle daughter looks just like my dad in the face. Her smart-ass mischievous looks, some of the things that come out of her mouth, and some of the crap she gets into is 100 percent my father. She's always been that way. I try to remember my dad through things like that now. I know that she is here for that exact reason. She can give me peace in the middle of my chaos. I'm not sure how she does it. I know that my brother and her mother are both paying for my dad's raising, and I'm not going to lie; it makes me giggle. My dad would have gotten into so much trouble with her. They would have taken on the world. She would have taken on the world, and my dad would have taken the blame and funded her adventures, that is. The thought of that while I type this makes me smile.

I've been seeing a guy for five years. I met him at work while working at a county jail, and we matched sarcasm. Not many men can do that. Most find me a stand-offish bitch. (I'm completely ok with that.) It takes a long time to break through the wall that I've worked so hard to surround myself with. We've had our problems, but I'm completely in love with him. I know I'm a lot to take on, but we couldn't stay away from each other. Our relationship moves at a snail's pace for one reason or another, but I can't imagine my life without him. It's a challenge, and it is constant work for us both. When I'm with him I feel peace, and that has to be worth something. It's like warm tea and your favorite blanket. My breaths automatically sync up to his when he's in the same room. I'm not sure if marriage will ever happen, but I hope one day it does. My dad would have liked him. He would have loved my dad. I don't know if I'll ever let him meet my mother. I know I'm nothing like her, but I don't think I want him to see that part of my life. The parents of mine he will know will be Jack and Kathy.

My brother went on to go to paramedic school, and he's done great with it. I'm jealous of his knowledge. It seems like he knows about anything that I'm currently struggling with at the time. He had a long-term relationship that gave him two more children. Luckily, she's a good mom and takes good care of my niece and nephew. He's a good dad and does the "Weekend Dad" thing. He's always shared his kids with me. He knew I wanted to be a mom. He works long hours during the week, but we keep in touch, and we're always there for each other if we need to be. When the dark cloud comes back over my head, he's still the first one I call.

He reminds me of my dad so much. He looks like my dad. When I go through pictures of my dad in younger days, I can really see it. He has my dad's hands. They're calloused and freckled and have years of hard work in them. He has a love for kids and animals like my dad did. He's saved a few of both. He's a bigger guy than my dad was, so seeing that soft side of him that he inherited from my dad is comical at times. His temper has calmed down a bit since he became a father. I'm finally used to it, but seeing my brother be a dad was totally wild to experience. That gruff, abrasive guy became a diaper-changing cuddle bug. Tea parties and Spiderman are a regular at his place now. I never thought I'd see that.

I rarely speak to my mother. She's oxygen dependent and in a wheelchair. She actually burned the house down that dad left while smoking with her oxygen on. As with anything in life, she made it out fine, but destroyed our childhood keepsakes. She now lives in a trailer on the outside of the same tiny town. She's not left her place in a couple of years unless it's to go to the hospital. I will call her about once a month, but that's as much as I can do right now. She doesn't remember a good part of our conversations, or that I've even called because she's so hypoxic most of the time. She has a home care aide that comes in for a few hours every day. My brother has done more than his share of making sure she's ok. I know she loves her grandchildren, but they are always supervised and don't stay long. I think she knows deep down in her heart why, even though she won't admit it. Again, she's doing the finding Jesus thing. I know in her head, she's been forgiven, which is fine. Ben and I can't forget though.

I have made some really great friends in my nursing career. I'm not sure how much longer I can physically do it, but I'm trying my best. I've developed a work family from places where I've worked; some will text me and check on me often. I've learned that blood doesn't make a family. Family are the people that stick around while you are going through hell. They are your cheerleaders. They are your comfort. They are your home when you need one.

Hannah and I reconnected and even lived together for a bit. She has two boys that are adorable. She seems to be happy with her life, and I'm glad. Julia lives in the same town and is still as fancy as she was all those years ago. I still think I could call her, and she'd do what she could for me. Again, friends turned into family. She'll always be a comfort to me in some way.

I've not spoken to Kayla in years, but I do know she has two little boys and works full time as a therapist. Life changes and gets busy, but I'm thankful for all the times she was in my life. I'm sure she's thriving. She always has.

Jack and Kathy are still very much in my life. It's where I go when I need guidance. They have an open door policy, and I can walk through their door at any time. They've adopted me from day one, and I feel like I belong there. Jack kept his word. He will always be my "Stand-in Dad."

Ms. D, the legend, has retired and is enjoying it. I don't talk to her as much as I'd like to, but we do get together for dinner occasionally. She's gotten to travel and do all the things that people do when they retire. She deserves to do that and so much more. I truly believe that she is the reason I'm still hanging out on this planet. She's definitely the reason I'm a nurse. I'll always be grateful for everything she did when everyone else would have let me melt.

I found out a few years ago that Joey died about seven years after he raped me. I don't really know what happened, but I ran across a Facebook page that was in memory of him. He had gotten married and had a son before he died. I hope his son is being raised by a strong woman who teaches him to respect women. I find it unfair that he moved on and got to have a family. I hope his son does well in life. No one should pay for the sins of their parents. I'm not sorry he's dead though.

I never went to the police. Although I can still hear everyone telling me what a mistake that was, it was what was right for me—my choice. If I had had to have gone through a rape kit at that point, I would have fractured into a million pieces. I don't regret my decision, because I did what I needed to do to survive at the time. Of course this has changed me, and it made me hard to love. I was the first to fight for a long time. It made me very confrontational. I had just decided I wasn't going to be treated wrongly again by anyone. Especially a man.

I've learned through trial and error. Mostly error—that you have to deal with your past before you put it away or it always follows you. I see a psychologist regularly, and I'm on meds for panic attacks and depression. It took me developing a habit of cutting myself and a lot of suicidal ideation to finally give in and go. I'm making progress, but it's an everyday battle. Some days are setbacks, but I wake up the next day and keep going forward. I'm using the tools I've been taught daily to make it through life. This world can be a scary place, but you have to keep going. My temper is much better than it has been in the past. Age, therapy, and meds have all helped me in that.

Life really is a rollercoaster. You just have to hold on and keep going. It gets easier. I hope that writing all this out gives me closure and peace. I deserve both of those. Hopefully, this helps someone reading it. You can put a life back together that's been shattered. It's not easy, but there are good people and things in this world. The hard part is learning to run towards them instead of away from them.

www.ingramcontent.com/pod-product-compliance
Ingram Content Group UK Ltd.
Pitfield, Milton Keynes, MK11 3LW, UK
UKHW022217230426
12048UKWH00016BA/899